MY JOURNEY

First Published in 2021

Beyond The Vale Publishing

Bonga Sibulele Makholwa

MY JOURNEY- A REMINDER TO SELF

"STEP INTO THE OF FIRE OF SELF DISCOVERY,
THIS FIRE WILL NOT BURN YOU. IT WILL
BURN WHAT YOU ARE NOT" - MOOJI

Contents

6

Dedication

When I began this journey of reminding myself of me, I could sense that I would be that weird person.

All my life, I've always wondered why I have been the "outside" or the one where it doesn't make sense, the "fool" to make you dream but never the one to make you realize it. The one who has to always take the fall, the one who has to be the bigger man. The one who sees the real game and has to sacrifice the Queen.

It is my turn now. My turn to express that which I seek to experience but I still have to humble myself.

Is this bigger than me? Have I gone much further than I am equipped to go?

I've always felt I have incarnated before my time. Yet my ego always reminded me to humble myself. Why?

To come back and redo what you have perfected with no knowledge that you have perfected it!?

It is truly an art.

It is art that I wish to portray to you.

An art of life

An art of crying.

An art I call my journey.

I stand on the shoulders of giants throughout history. I cannot name them yet their words echo through Our journey.

Our journey is one and I am only repeating what the masters before me and you had come to manifest. Tough were the levels of consciousness yet they prevailed. Now you and me stand here with nothing but excuses.

Here is a reminder.

From the masters to the masters.

In this book I acknowledge my self.

I acknowledge that which I have feared my whole life.

To stop playing small and give it my All.

I am All in The All and The All in All after all.

To Katego More, my friend this one is for you, rest easy my friend, your journey has just started.

My Journey

Introduction

In your journey day after day the sun rises and sets;
Night after night the moon appears and disappears.

And;

Though night and day come to pass, nothing seems to change.

Yet still at every moment when you look back, everything seems to have changed.

You know;

There comes a time when you have to break away from the crowd, and come back to Self.

A time to remember who You are, instead of what you have been told you are.

A time when your inner voice is louder than the outside noises. Truth is;

Throughout your whole life you will always experience a moment;

this moment, fleeting yet ever present, will always be now here yet again no where.

And through all this 'time and space' in this moment, there is no where to go but now here.

This moment always now here but no where;
is all that ever was, is all that ever will be and all that ever is.

In this moment you may try to escape, for the moment you may seem to be in the 'time and space' of the what was.

For the moment you may seem to be in the 'time and space' of is to be.

Yet in this moment, in that moment, in those moments, in all moments and in the moment, all that was and all that will be;

is truly all that is, now here yet no where;
in this moment, in that moment, in those moments, in all moments.

This moment; always remaining with you wherever you may seem to go.
This moment; always staying with you wherever you may seem to be.

This moment; always within you with you wherever you are.
This moment; always here now yet no where.
This moment; which you can feel yet cannot seem to touch.
This moment; which you can observe yet cannot seem to perceive.
This moment; which you can hear yet cannot seem to understand.

This moment; has always been here, with you.

Yes;
In that moment, in those moments and in all moments.
It has always been the only moment.

Through the time and space within you, there only exists this moment.
This moment is always the beginning, this moment is always the ending.

In every moment, this moment is always beginning the ending and ending the beginning;
A truly endless beginning, this moment cannot begin, this moment cannot end, this moment is all that is.

This moment, is that moment,
This moment, is those moments,
This moment, is all moments,
And the only moment.

This moment; is Your journey.
And,
To whom who can hear; understand.
To whom who can see; observe.
To whom who can think; imagine.
To whom who can seek; find.
To whom who can feel; experience.
To whom who wants; have.
To whom who is; be.

And so;
To whom the consciousness is awakened, the God within comes out and plays.
Yet still, there come many moments in the journey where;
To whom the consciousness is asleep, the gods without come in and control.

Yet here and now, all you know is;

You awakened to a life.
You awakened to a moment in eternity.

In the movement you became still, yet still, in the stillness you were moving.

Where do you go?
Left, where nothing is right?
Or
Right, where nothing is left?

Think about it;

Now think about it.

You know;
sometimes you may find the answer in the question, and sometimes you never know, you may find the question in the answer.

Simply put, you may question your answers to actually answer your question.

This is The journey, This is Our journey, This is Your journey and This is My journey.

And ;
In this journey lay forth an infinity of possibilities, an unlimited birth of experiences, within and without, an expression of creation creating.

Breathe.
Be still.
Your journey requires You.

The Dilemma

You have spent most of your life in the search for answers and
truth, though you saw you never actually perceived,
Though you heard you never actually listened.

It has never hit you that you looked far beyond that which actually is.
You looked outside and all you could do is dream, but I tell you the truth, look within and awaken.

For too long you have depended on another to walk the path for you in hope that they will reach the destination for you.

For too long you have given your power to other beings in hope that they will save you.

For too long you have lived the life defined by others in hope that you will have succeeded.

For too long you have ignored the inner voice in hope that the outside noises are the right guides.

And for too long you have denied yourself in order to be accepted in a world that was never meant to be perfected.

You know;
In a world that tries its utmost best day and night to make you everybody else,
to stand up and be You is truly perfection.

In a world that tries its utmost best day and night to make you chase everything,
to stand and be still is truly perfection.

In a world that tries its utmost day and night to make you look outside and dream,
to stand looking within and awaken is truly perfection.

Truly speaking;
Perfection is when Spirit lives through you and you live through Spirit.

It is thus the love of the Spirit within you that will always get you to the destination of your creation,
and that the fear of the gods without will always get you to the destination of your reaction.

So then;
To whom the consciousness is awakened, the Spirit within comes out to play.
To whom consciousness is asleep, the gods without come in and control.

Remember;
In this life,
only you can live this life of yours;
only you can walk the path which you please to go;
only you can determine the destiny of your life;
only you can truly judge the life you live; only you can be you;
only you have the chance to be you; only you can live for you.

IT

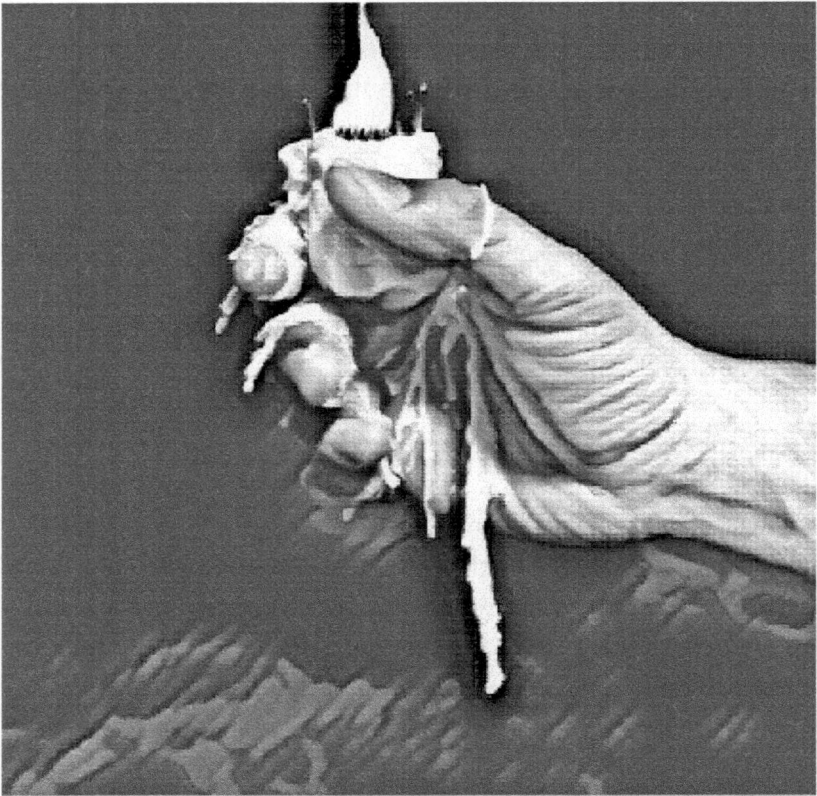

In us, without us, beside us, before us, after us;
it creates that which is in us,
it creates that which is reflected without,
it creates that which is always beside us,
it creates that which is before us,
it creates that which will come after us.

It is neither this path or that path,
it is neither the right path or the wrong path,
it is neither the only path or no path at all.

It is this path and that path,
it is the right and the wrong path,
it is the only path and every path.

An expression of all that is;
creating creation to create, creation being all that is, moving into, through and out of form into more creation, all that is, is created.

A creation creating creation, life moving into more life, an experience of experience, everything is;
a creation creating creation, life moving into more life, an experience of experience.

Who are you? You are The All in All and All in The All.

What are you? You are All that is, moving into, through and out of form.

How are you? You are the creator creating creation and creation creating the creator is how you are.

When are you? You are now, even before and after.

Where are you? You are no where yet now here.

Why are you? You are because you are.

On: Thoughts, words and Actions

In your journey through the incarnation of physical human form you have walked through depths of the illusion of separation.

You found yourself lost in a world that is no where but now here, yet in this world you experience an illusion of your consciousness, thoughts, and feelings as separate from all that is.

This illusion of separation from yourself only leads you into experiencing a self that is not You.

In your journey through the space and time of thought; you experience but a vast ocean of potential expressions of experience.

Through you comes the treasure of life becoming all that is, all in you moving into, through and out of form into the eternal creation.

You need to remember;

You are the vast space and time into which thoughts arise, pass and go.
Thoughts cannot be, except through you.

A creation of the creator creating in this moment and every moment.

Thoughts;
the vast creating form of creation creating yet only a part of the creator creating creation;
is but only the potential of creation experienced, moving into, through and out of form as you choose to experience them, to arise or pass or go.

From thoughts arises the life that is projected into physical form manifested;
a constant flow of life moving into, through and out of form it is a constant creation creating.

From the unseen; thought is but the creator of the seen, and yet still, from the seen; thought is but the creator of the unseen.

From the beginning, thought is but the creator of the ending, and yet still, from the ending, thought is but the creator of the beginning.

From life, thought is but the creator of death, and yet still, thought is but the creator of life.

From the cause, thought is but the creator of the effect, and yet still, from the effect, thought is but the creator of the cause.

Thought is that which flows through you, a constant creation of creation creating, an eternal moment of potential;

You can allow them to arise or pass or go through you into all that is.

It is that to whom consciousness is awakened;
the creator within freely expands its wand of creation into all that is;
and it is so that to whom consciousness is asleep;
the creating creations without come in, and control the creation with the wand that has become the cage into which all that is, is not.

Through thought, the path that arises is neither the wrong nor the right path, but only the destination to which you find that in every right path there is a wrong path and in every wrong path there is a right path.

There are but many ways up the mountain, there are only paths into which you can climb, a vast canvas into which you project each step as you create your path into the mountain of life.

Thought, through your journey into the human physical form;
is the creation creating creation, moving into, through and out of form into more thoughts of creation creating creation.

You, the consciousness, energy, observer, creator;
Is the vast space and time in eternity which thoughts come to rise and move through the canvas of the creator and project experience through expression.

It is through thought that the life force in you gives birth to the forces of life for you, like a seed in the soil that gives birth to the sprout in roots, which moves into, through and out of form into a tree.

In its essence, an unmoved mover yet still a moved un-mover; It is the creation creating creation that is constantly projecting expressions of itself through the experience of moving into, through and out of form within you.

Thought; it is the wand of creation and the creation of magic.

Thoughts come and go, you either give birth to their experience or watch them pass as they come and go.

In your journey in human form thoughts became words, and soon moving into, through and out of form those words became actions.

In your journey in human form actions become habits, and soon moving into, through and out of form those habits became values.

In your journey in human form values became destiny, and soon moving into, through and out of form that destiny became all that is.

In your journey you are the vast space into which thoughts give birth to the experience of expression.

So;
When each moment manifests in your reality, begin to be fully conscious, and to be conscious is to be aware, and to be aware is to be alive.

Be alive in the being in you, each thought, word and action in alignment with what you want to express and experience.

Do linger in your thoughts but be stable in your words and actions, find balance in the flow from one state to another and you will arrive where you so envied to be.

When you find yourself at war with your thoughts, look upon your words and actions to gain peace.

Do this each moment, remember this in every moment and be this in all moments.

Behind the vale of your thoughts, words and actions is your being.
And what you are being in thought, in word, in action manifests into the vale of life.

And even when these states of being are not in alignment; with a constant flow these states become aligned.

It is you who readily dwells in each state of being, causing and effecting the reality you continue to experience.

Your life is always in your thoughts, words and actions;

Take it back and reclaim your being.

If you are to manifest any reality in your journey, bring forth change in your thoughts, words, and actions.

No one can think for you, no one can say it for you and no one can act upon it for you.

No one can but you, can.

And the sooner you begin to realize this, the sooner you end your constant suffering.

Remember;

When you give your power to create away, the reality that manifests will surely be one that is of others thinking, words and actions.

And so;

When you take your power to create back, the reality that manifests will surely be one that is of your thinking, words and actions.

In these two pathways, we choose how life must go on for each, whether you are rowing the boat or just sitting there, the waters will continue to move.

To consciously or to unconsciously create is the question.

Thoughts, words and actions are but your tools to unlock your innermost experience.

It is not an easy journey, alignment with your innermost thoughts, words, actions will be needed on constant basis.

At each moment you have to separate yourself; observe, and steer yourself where you want to express your experience.

Use each moment of consciousness to remind yourself who you are;
in whatever experience you feel, be conscious that you have the tools to become all that you seek to experience.

Stop limiting yourself, for a moment let go of all complaining, and see your life as what it truly is.

A beautiful creation you give yourself, a journey only you can understand and walk, a peace and serenity only you can experience.

Give yourself this gift, use this "cage" you have imprisoned yourself in for so long.

You must be patient in your pursuit, calm in your expectations, and efficient in your actions.

On: Laws That Govern

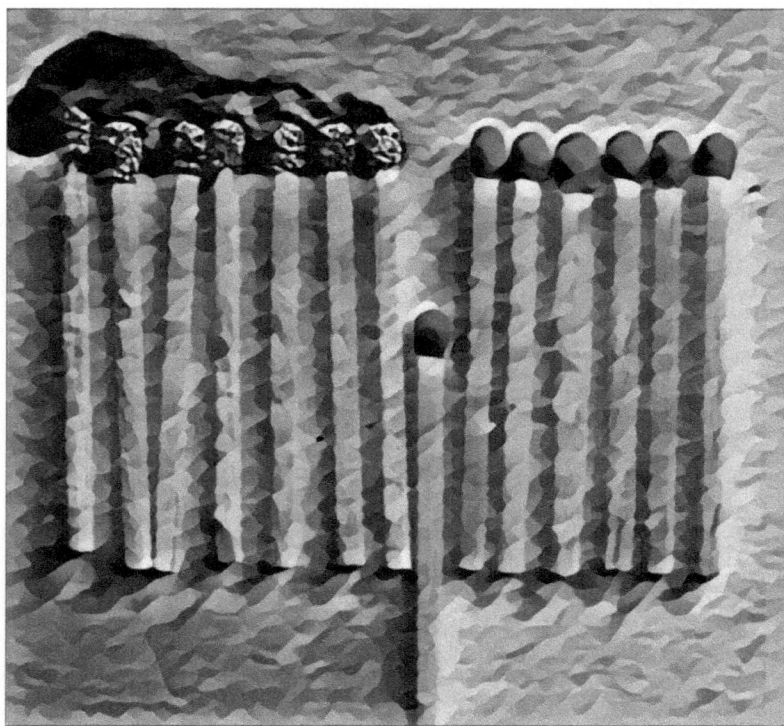

There is law that governs you and all that it is;

From the mental structure of your universe, to the physical manifestation you see.

All manifestation in life springs forth from the mental, conscious, subconscious realm of existence.

The one place in which belief is constructed;
The one place in which habits are formed;
The one place in which decisions are reached;
The one place which all your life comes from.

You, you are that place, and life is but a mirror reflecting the perceiver.

So then;

Look upon the cause and you will find the effect.
Look within your Self and you will find the universe.
Look through stillness and you will find movement.
Look at this and you will find that.

All the things in life that you define as this and that, are but fruits of the same tree;
The difference in them is that they are uniquely similar.

Everything is matter, everything is energy and everything is spirit.

From spirit an eruption of energy can form any matter.
Behind matter is energy and behind it all is spirit.

Remember;
You are the creation that creates and so You are the creator that created;
You are the created creation and so You are the creation created;
The All creates All and All create The All.

The All created in All is made up of All created in The All, The All created in All comes from All created in The All, All created in The All return to The All created in All.

It is thus All created in The All are made up of The All created in All, All created in The All come from The All created in All, All created in The All return to The All created in All.

You are All that is, now and every moment You always are;
You are All that ever was, now and every moment You always were;
You are All that ever will be, now and every moment You will always be.

You are All that is, and so All that is, You are.

What You are created what You were and thus what You are will create what You will be.

You are the seed of life, You are the beginning and the ending,
life cannot be, except through You.

What I am, You are.

You are the Alpha and the Omega in the reality that is called life,
between thoughts and actions lay forth life.

Through the depths of searching for Spirit, You find; but
yourself.
Through the horizons of searching for yourself, you find; but
Spirit.

Life unfolds before you just as you unfold before life,
creation creating creation,

The cause of life is you and the effect of life is you,
an experience of being,
creating more being of experience,
an expression of life that seems no where but now here.

In the land of conscious physical life, deep beneath the shadows
of the light shining through space and time;

behind the vale of the seen is the unseen,
behind the vale of the physical is the non-physical,
behind the vale of creation is the creator,
behind the vale of the human you are is Spirit within.

It is the cause of the unseen, that creates the effect of the seen.
It is the cause of the non-physical, that creates the effect of the physical.
It is the cause of the creator, that creates the effect of the creation.
It is the cause of the Spirit within, that creates the effect of the human you are.

On: Loving Self

I remember the times you used to dream of the happily ever after;
yet at moment after moment you seem to be experiencing happily never after.

Funny how happily ever after is out there and not in here.

Funny how you cannot seem to love yourself perfectly; yet at some point you were able to love an imperfect soul so perfectly.

Yet I say to you;

Learn to give yourself what you would give another.

Remember;
love is unconditional, love does not possess but appreciates, love is always unlimited in its giving.

And remind yourself;
You are Love,
for you are unconditional in being, you cannot possess another yet can but only appreciate, you are unlimited in giving of yourself always.

I know;
Sometimes you hide what's inside, and play to the audience.
Yet it all gets too much when you should be smiling yet your tears keep bringing up rivers down the valleys of your cheeks.

I say to you, breathe.

Breathe and ask yourself, how long till I get tired of being tired. It is a draining experience to always be somebody else for everyone else.

Rarely do you find yourself being you for you.

Its always;

I will be this for my parents,
I will be that for my God,
I will be this for my country,
I will be that for my children. The list can go on and on, yet You never include You in Your life.

Most of your time you spend thinking about other people, other experiences which you yourself would not want, is it because you can't see what you are or is it because others can't see what you are?

Breathe, close your eyes, and open them with the awareness that you are a seer/watcher, open them with the consciousness that you are a Creator.

I repeat.
Learn to give yourself what you would give another.

That love, this happiness.

That wholeness, this perfection.
That appreciation, that freedom to be.

Begin to give yourself these pleasures, remember to drink upon these waters, and start to manifest what love is.

Remember and remind yourself to;
Love yourself with all your mind, love yourself with all your heart, love yourself with all your soul.

For this is the way and the life;
no one can be the creator creating creation except through being creation creating the creator, with all your soul loving yourself, with all your heart loving yourself, with all your mind loving yourself.

It is only then that you can love your reflections, each one of them unique just like you, All in The All and The All in All.

You are The All and All are reflections, everything is; reflections in you.

And only when You have learnt to love yourself with all your mind, can you be able to love your reflections.
Only when you have learnt to love yourself with all your heart, can you be able to love your reflections,
and only when you have learnt to love yourself with all your soul, can you be able to love your reflection.
You are but the whole in a part, you are but a part in the whole.

You are but the ocean in a drop, you are but a drop in the ocean.

You are but the one in everything, you are but the everything in one.
You are but the beginning in the ending, you are but the ending in the beginning.

You are but The All in All, you are but All in The All. You are that which is, all that is life. Life cannot be, except through you.

So;
Stop and take look at yourself, look deep within yourself, stop and wonder at this moment, take a look at yourself.

See what I see, a truly endless wonder that always is.

And remember;
To love, is to give all of yourself. To fear, is to restrict all of yourself.

Honour

Hark and know the place in you, the place where all that is resides.

An observer who now thinks, acts, feels and experiences the universe he expresses within himself.

Honour the true Self that You are;
In any thought, action, feeling and experience.

For in all these, always comes the duality within all life and things.

Look up in the sky and see a piece of infinity looking back at you,
look down and touch the earth connected to you,
look in front of you and see how nothing seems to change,
look back and see how everything has changed,
look within you and awaken to Yourself.

Stop and think this,
pause and act this,
be still,
feel this,
experience this.

Hark and know this place in you,
this place in you that thoughts, feelings, actions and experiences come into being.

Honour the true self that you are; the true self that thoughts, feelings, actions and experiences come into being.

Hark and know yourself. Honour yourself.

Honour;
This place where only you can choose your thoughts,
this place where only you can choose your feelings,
this place where only you can choose your actions,
this place where only you can choose your experience.

This place is now and this place is you.

Remember;
Behind the thoughts there is but an expresser,
Behind the feelings there is but an expresser,
behind the actions there is but an expresser,
and so behind the experiences there is but an expresser.

This expresser, is the true self that you are.

And so behind all the thoughts, feelings, actions and experiences is where you choose to be yourself.

And who are you? You are no one. For when you are no one, you have but the power to be anyone.

And what are you? You are nothing. For when you are nothing, you have but the power to be anything.

And where are you? You are nowhere. For when you are nowhere, you have but the power to be anywhere.

So then;
Let your thoughts come as you direct them with your feelings, actions and experiences, yet hark and know who you are.

Let your feelings come as you direct them with your actions, experience and thoughts, yet hark and remember what you are. This is the life and the way, through all life and every way, there is an expresser behind all that is.

Yes.
At times you seek to find the next joyful moment, the final complete reality of your inner most being.

That moment that will be the finishing touch to the move, this moment that has been the build up to it all, that moment that the story has been written for, this moment that has been all that is, that moment that is all there is.

Yet take this moment that you are witnessing.

Stop and take a moment to look at this moment, stop and count this moment, see that it is the only moment.

Know that it is the moment, the moment in which you determine the moment.

Feel yourself naked, see yourself stripped, know yourself as transparent and experience yourself as pure.

Stand still and know that you are Spirit.

You have played small, in the big leagues you acted a part relegated in itself,
yet in the competition of expression, you have no choice but to play.

Play, hark, know, and experience yourself as The All in All and All in The All.

You have no choice but this.

There is no other game to play,
there is no other life to die for,
there is no other dream to become reality,
and there is no other answer to our question.

This again, your only dilemma, to be yourself or to live as everybody else?

Where do you go?
Left, where nothing is right?
Or
Right, where nothing is left?

Think about it though; do you go through life or what you call all that is, as an automated source of experience and expression?

And if so and not so,
do you consciously go through that life or what you call all that is, as a creative source of experience and expression?

Stop and ask yourself these questions,
hark and know the answers that lay within.

Move forth and begin to witness the answer that you are!

You tangle yourself in the infinite eternity that you are,
you may try to make sense of the mystery you seem to be,
you may unravel the perfectness that you have always been,
and you may even witness, express, and experience you as the only moment that has always been here now.

Yet again, stop.

Stop and take a good look at this wonder that you are,
pause and reflect at this perfection that you are,
hark and understand this simplicity you reflect,
slowly and steadily you will control this wheel of destiny,
swiftly and connected you will forever be engraved in this dream that has become a reality.

God and human you shall be towards all that is.

This, your only solution to your dilemma,
is your journey.

This, your only road to your destination,
is your journey.

This, your only reality to your dream,
 is the journey.

And this, your only thought, feeling, expression and experience;
is your path.

On: Religion

You seek outside,
You belittled yourself,
You did not think beyond what you are told for a very long time.

Hark and know;
No one is coming to save you,
no one is coming to begin life for you,

no one is coming to end life for you,
no one is going to create life for you,
no one is going to destroy life for you,
no one is going to cause life for you,
no one is going to effect life for you,
no one is going to live life for you,
no one is going to die in life for you,
no one is going to be you for you,
no one can.

No one but You can;

Save yourself; begin life for yourself; end life for yourself;
create life for yourself; destroy life for yourself; cause life for
yourself; effect life for yourself; live life for yourself; die in life
for yourself; be you for yourself.

So then;
Be careful that your religion does not blind you from Spirit.

Be careful that your religion does not hide you from Yourself.

Be careful that your religion does not alienate you from your
fellow man.

Again;
Do not rebel against religion, it has been a great leap to coming
back to yourself.

It has played its part in your remembering of your true nature.

You know now;

Spirit as you imagine deep in your heart, is unconceivable through this mind of yours;

Yet you experience Spirit at all moments and may try to describe the true nature of Creator.

Can you take Self and hold it?

You know;

Truly speaking, there is this script that you seem to have to follow, a part you have to portray to the Artist.

And;
As it is, truly speaking religion is at its best when it makes you question yourself, question whether this world you find yourself in is all there is.

Truly speaking religion is at its worst when it makes you think you already know all there is to know, to think you already have it all figured out.

In this experience that you find yourself in;

There is but a vast canvas moving into all that is here now and always.

The only truth you know is what you experience.
The only guide you know is what you experience and the only world you know is what you experience.

Experience comes from you and lives through you.

You are that which you seek.

And so;
Let religion go and arrive at Spirit.

You are Spirit, and that which you seek to be greater than you, is but You.

Spirit on a human being's journey, Spirit experiencing All, our journey leads to one destination.

For;
Spirit will never burn yet it burns.

It is not out there but in you, it is you.

Undress all the conditioning through life and your Spirit.

Talk to Spirit, talk to yourself, it is a conversation with God.

So then;

When I speak, hark my words;

'My Children, who art in Heaven, hallowed is your name (for you are energy, spirit).

Your kingdom (Your life) comes and your will is done, on earth as it is in heaven (in thoughts, in soul and in spirit).

You are given this day your daily bread, and you are forgiven your debts and your trespasses, exactly to the degree that you have forgiven those who trespass against you. (The All is in All and All are in The All. You are One, therefore do unto others as it would be done to you).

Lead your Self not into temptation (separation from what you are: God);

but deliver your Self from the evils you have created (In thought, word, and deed)

For thine is the Kingdom, and the Power, and the Glory, forever and ever, it shall be. '

So;

Go on;

Make your own decisions, have your own thoughts, create your own experiences, and only then can you begin to live.

Go on;

let go of their beliefs and believe your experience, release the "out there" and awake in the "in here", come back to yourself and witness Spirit living through you.
You are the Alpha and the Omega in the reality that is called life; between thoughts and actions lay forth life.

In this journey beyond the infinitely eternal, remember;
You are energy, You are consciousness, You are spirit on a human being's journey.

You are not merely a part in the whole, You are the whole in a part.

In this journey beyond the infinitely eternal, remember;
You are energy, You are consciousness, You are spirit on a human being's journey.

You are not merely a drop in the ocean, You are the whole ocean in a drop.

Through the depths of searching for God, You find; but yourself.
Through the horizons of searching for yourself, you find; but God.

He who looks outside can only dream.
Yet
He who looks within will always awaken.

And;

"What is the point in having your own thoughts, words, actions and feelings if you are to live someone else's thoughts, words, actions and feelings? "

This; your only dilemma, the courage to be yourself or to live as everybody else.

To listen to the silence from within and find your voice.
Or
To hear the voices from outside and lose the silenced peace.

This silence, this voice, this happiness;
is Me.
And when You seek Me outside Yourself, You can only dream about Me.
Yet still;
When You seek Me within You, You will always awaken.

Didn't I tell ye are God's.

When You do not speak, listen to your silence! And when You speak, hark your words, thoughts, feelings and actions.

On: Death

You only realize how life is a passing wave in the ocean of eternity a little too late.

During the present it seems the destination is nowhere reachable, and a far distance always seems to beckon you right after you surpass another.

Only when the wave has immersed into the ocean, do you become conscious that you are only a visitor to this shore called life.

Only when life has awoken its twin, do you start to appreciate its preciousness.

Only when there is no more moments, do you begin to know the value of any and all moments.

It is a reminder of your illusion.

Yet;

Stop and wonder at the journey you have walked, be conscious of the journey you are walking, and give thanks to the destination that lies ahead.

In life you will find death, it is a sleep you cannot avoid, and I tell you truth, in death, you will find life, it is an awakening you cannot escape.

Life is the "Here" you cannot avoid and Death is the "There" you cannot escape.

Between Here and There is what you are.

You will continue moving from here to there.

Know that this Here; is only another wave passing in the ocean.

Understand that There; is only another night in days to come.

When you leave your body in this plane of existence, you arrive in spirit in another plane of existence.

When spirit is embarking on a human being's journey, it is a moment.

A moment to experience the extremes of duality,
a moment to experience the cause and effects of your journey,
a moment to experience the depths of opposites.

This moment is an ecstasy which brings you to You.

When spirit leaves the body; it is so that it can arrive at a new destination.

The conditions and circumstances in which it consciously or unconsciously created no longer served its experience.

It has run its lap and it is time to refuel.

Many roads lay forth before you; paths yet to be paved, and destinations yet to be reached.

This life is a moment in you; a moment for you and source to experience expression.

You will leave with only what you have expressed and experienced, back to you, returning to source; it is all we are here to do.

To Express, to Experience.
And so;

In death find rest, find that last long breathe to contemplate the journey to be travelled.

Do not fear; for fear is for the world you leave behind.

Know that the burden has been lifted; understand that the suffering has
ended; the time to reflect has come.

It is only a break in a marathon; a marathon back to knowing yourself.

An endless beginning, moving into, through, and out of form.
God living out loud is the beat you are moving at.

You cannot not be, like in a dream you will leave this world and plane of existence;
arriving at a new world and plane of existence you will continue to create your journey.

Remember;

Fear for death is for those you leave behind in this world; And a fear only because of being unconscious of the reality that spirit moves into and out of form.

Attach yourself to the spirit of a human and you will remember that you are never separated. In this moment, in that moment, and in all moments you will always be attached.

For you are everything, and everything comes from everything and so everything returns to everything.
The All is in All and All are in The All.

Remember;

You and Me are not separated; yet hold dear to the view that Spirit is looking through you.

This view of experience is yours to harness and cultivate; ever growing in its knowing of self, it goes on and on remembering itself.

Through life and out of death, it begins to remember itself as creation.

Slowly through this journey it moves its experience through expression.

Each time leaving the body, experience is its lingering shadow; Each time arriving in a new body, expression is its lingering shadow.

Life is but a journey whose destination is now-here.
And;

This is the canvas on which you have chosen to create your own experience.

Here now is where you begin to consciously create that which you long to express.

You have chosen this journey to remember yourself.

To remember parts of you that you have long forgotten, parts still and always within you yet never tapped into.

Therefore go on and live.
For when death knocks, another life awaits.

On: Dreams

There is a reality or plane of existence that you keep visiting.

Everyday without fail; your soul leaves the body and arrives at the 'astral' plane.

Many can recollect pieces when coming back and many more cannot recall anything.

Yet each human knows of dreaming or deep sleep as some say.
Funny how you never touch upon the things that affect you, the things that you experience everyday,
Yet when you wake up you go back to an even deeper sleep.

Yet I say;
Look upon your dreams to understand your creative force.

Look upon your dreams to observe force of life create.

Look upon your dreams to feel vibration at its lowest and highest.

Look upon your dreams to connect to Self and All.

Look upon your dreams to remind you who You are.

The dream world is a canvas;
our consciousness the paint that brings life,
our thoughts are but the pencil which drafts,
our words are but the charcoal which gives boldness,

our actions are but the pastel that gives identity,
and our feelings are but the masterpiece that completes the
incomplete.

Your dreams are but;
Another chance for you to dance to the beat of life.
Another plane of existence for you to create more of life.

It is another life in life,
A consciousness, a being, a life.

For You can never rest, you are All that is;
You cannot not be, you are just;
Moving into, through, and out of form into what is.

At every moment you always are; at every conceivable moment
your journey does not end.

At your lowest and at your highest, you always are.

Remember;
You are the creator, creating, creation.
You are the creator;
You are creating;
You are creation.

In this moment, in that moment, in those moments and in all
moments you never cease to be.

You are not this body, your journey does not end here on earth.

The body is a vehicle for this plane of existence;
love and express its senses, like you would in your astral body.

Lighter and sure of your decisions, manifestation using but the
tools you already have;
Thoughts, words, actions and feelings.

And when you awake you may find;
This plane of existence may be coarse in its nature;
it may be slow in its manifestation of your creation;
it may be complicated in its simplicity.

Yet know and stand firm in your creation and life will beat to
your dance.

Do not be afraid and fear what you behold. It is what you are.

Thoughts, words, actions, feelings, death, life, dreams, the
things that truly affect your life are but a child with no mother
and no father.

You will keep blaming this and that for your life, you will keep
longing for this and that, you will keep not having enough of
this and that, and you will keep not having this and that.

And until you begin to look within, observe ourselves create life, change your patterns and habits that keep trapping you; will you begin to live life again.

Through dreams, through life and through death.

You dream, and you will live and die in the dream,
You live, and you will die and dream in this life,
You die, and you will dream and live in the death.

To My Generation

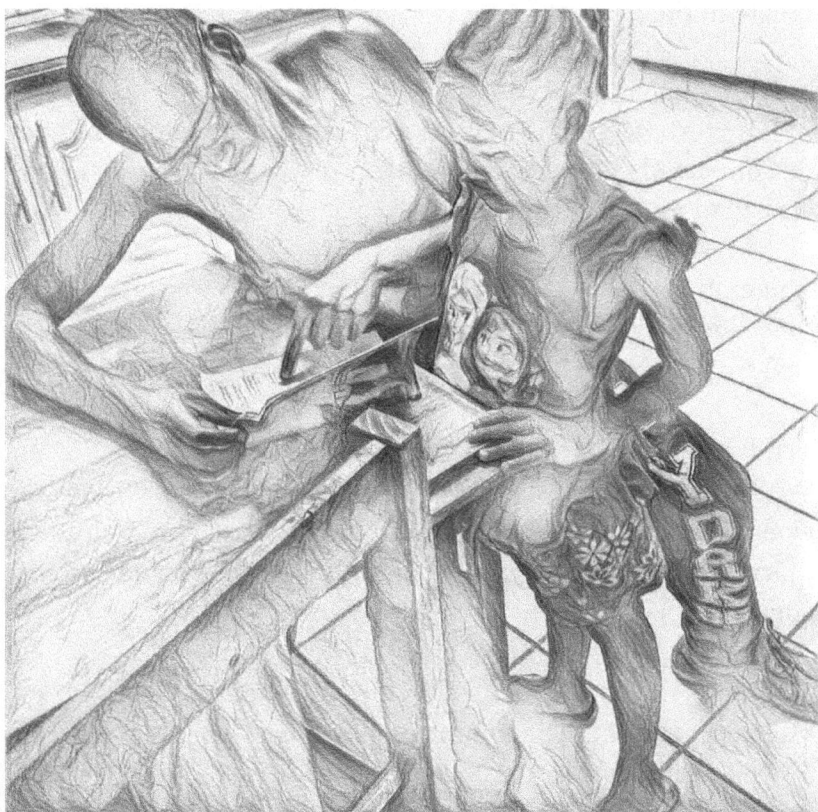

We may choose to dwell in the chains of the past, yet in its shadows will we continue to chase.

We may choose to dwell in the cages of the future, yet in its illusion will we continue to dream.

Yet we may choose to dwell in the kingdom of the present;
the past we will create in the present, and the future we will create in the present.

Tell me;
'Who were we before race separated us, before religion disconnected us, before politics divided us, and wealth classified us?'

Remember;
'We can easily forgive a child who is afraid of the dark, but the real tragedy of life is when men are afraid of the light'.

Truth is;
We have forgotten that; we are one with everything and everyone, we are pieces of a great puzzle and a great puzzle in pieces, each piece by itself making the whole bigger picture complete.

Truth is;
To fear Spirit, is the beginning of all ignorance.
To be Spirit, is the beginning of all wisdom.

It is true;
Often at times it falls upon a generation to become great.
We can be that generation, we are that generation.

The generation in which the inner voice is louder than the outer opinions,
The generation in which the power of love overcomes the love of power,
The generation in which You are Me and I am You.

A generation in which we know that there are never victims, but just Creators.

A generation in which every light that shines, knows it lightens its path, and yet others too.

A generation that You and Me can create, is creating; for we are the creation that creates.

Therefore;
'In a society that has destroyed all adventure, the only adventure left is to destroy that society,'

If we are waiting on God to solve our problems, our wait will be forever;
For God did Her part long ago, fulfilled the biggest promise of unlimited potential.

We could not help but get caught up in the crowd, yet there came a time and space where we found ourselves no further than the crowd.

A time and space seemingly apart, but here and now.
Where will we go?
left, where nothing is right?
or
right, where nothing is left?

We go no where;
We go now here;
We be still and know we are The All in All and All in The All.

Remember;
It takes simplicity to know sophistication.

It takes a moment to determine eternity, yet still it takes eternity to determine a moment.

A moment is eternity expressed in a moment.

Eternity is a moment expressed in eternity.

An encircling beginning of the end and an encompassing ending of the beginning;
In us, through us and into all that is.

A vast canvas is what is in us.

A potential of All that is, is what is before us.
An experience of unlimited expression is what we are.
A creator creating creation is what we have always been.
Creation creating a creator is what we will always be.
A life within life is what we become.

This, our only destination.
An endless becoming of All that is,
a life in a life of creation creating a creator,
this, an unlimited expression of experience,
a potential of All that is, is what We are.

Look;
many roads lay before us, paths that are of our creation,
destinations found but yet to be travelled, a journey now, yet
no where.

Remember when we used to wonder at the everlasting song of
the morning birds whispering all that is good to our ears.

Maybe we've lost our way or maybe we are still going on in our
path.

We may even be going through hell to get to heaven.
We may even be going through heaven to get us to hell.

Yet where is our way?
What is our path?
Why should we go to hell?

How will we get to heaven?

It all doesn't matter;
maybe what should matter is only that we are on our way,
maybe what should matter is that the path is ours and ours
alone,
maybe what should matter is the hell we keep creating for
ourselves,
maybe what should matter is the heaven within ourselves.

Yet again;
it all doesn't matter,
what matters is what we decide to matter.

The way we decide what matters will determine the path in
which we cause ourselves to create an experience of hell or
heaven within us.

Remember this moment and all moments.

This moment, although passing yet always here, is all there is.
Moments have come to pass through us, yet this moment that
is always here, is here.

Before, Now and after it will always be here.
We create, we experience, and we become this moment always.

A moment in eternity is what we are; what we are is eternity in
a moment.

Yes;
we have belittled ourselves because of the past, we have played small because we fear the future.

Yet here is this moment.

This is the moment that created the past, let it uplift us.

This is the moment that creates the future, let love rule it.

What are we waiting for? The next life? The next moment?
What if this 'next' never comes? And even if it does, what if it doesn't end our seeking?

What if life – and its fulfilment – is always NOW? Then, what's next?
Where do we go?

Left, where nothing is right.
Or
Right, where nothing is left.

And why should we even go?

We be still in this moment, be still and know we are Spirit.

Africa

In the land of Africa from which my journey began.
The land from which my path is unfolding.
The land where my destination will come to be.

I observe a young eagle, wounded by the physical cage that surrounded it.
Yet the cage no more but in the mind;

It continues to endlessly cast shackles that keep imprisoning it,

The more it resists, the more the chains persisted.

Yet there came a time where it let go,
and the more it let go,
the more it flowed,
freeing it,
new wings it manifested.

In the mind, the cage no more, in the physical, the cage no more.

Healed, the eagle experiences all that is.

Oh young Africa,
wounded by physical oppression, even when the oppression is no more.

In your mind it still continued to lure, endlessly casting shackles that manifested as the prison you keep yourself in.
The more you resist separation with separation;

the more separation will persist.

Yet here comes a time where you let go,
and the more you let go,
the more you flow with the power of the present and let go of
the shackles of the past.

Free you will be;
a new consciousness will manifest in you.

In your mind; the oppression no more.
In the physical, the oppression no more.

Healed, you will experience All that You are.

Oh Africa, where will you go?

left, where everything is right?
or
right, where everything is left?

Go forth and be yourself.
let your light shine amongst the land, brightening every path on
its way,
This light; lights up other lights without diminishing its own.
 It can never brighten its own light by diminishing another's.

Look;
I have walked in your footsteps;

strong and untethered were the foundations to guide our movement,
painful and caged were the roads that beckoned us.

Physically, we were prisoners in our own kingdom.

Mentally, we were slaves in our own Queendom.

Spiritually, we were unconscious of our own Godness.

Yet;
Here comes a time again, another chance to awaken within these dreams you've been sold.

A time to buy into the true reality you sleep through.

Physically you are enough, Mentally you are unlimited, Spiritually you are unconditional.

You cannot continue to think of yourself any less or even more.

You just are.

You are the spirit behind all life, the stuff that life is made of.

Now don't you dare even for a second think you are greater than any race.

Don't you even dare for a moment think you are beneath any race.

History has turned you into an ever fearful wanderer.

This time you have to overcome all that comes in front of you.

Not by force, not by aggression.

Gently my Africa, gently.

Gently will you conquer the fears within with awareness. Awareness that you are spirit, moving through, into, and out of form.

For slavery of the body and the mind are but a moment that has passed.

In a moment that had an infinity of pain, fear and limitation. Pleasure, Courage and Wealth was our craving.

Take this moment and be aware that you can move this experience into the expression you truly are.

This moment is not in the power of an invisible man in the sky who plays dice with lives of men.

This moment is right here within you, a power within you, not a power separate or outside of you.

Gently, my children, gently.

You are coming to your true consciousness,
you are arriving within your true experience,
you are at the gates of spirit.

Coming Back To Self

You are not the voice that speaks.

You are the presence that listens.

Start from a point of listening;
for all that you can speak is but an echo.

Be calm and know that you are God.
Be still and conscious of the universe residing within you.

Breathe; and let the echo of your silence play to divine beat.

Hark and know that You are safe.

Hark and know that You are unlimited.

Be still, Breathe and awaken to the God in You.

Do not be restless, do not suffocate yourself;
and be ignorant to the reflections that comes as life, to experience a feeling of being unsafe and limited, is not what it is.

It is not Me, it is not You.

It is not within you,

Yet it can only come through You,
It can only come through Me.

You find yourself at crossroads right now.

Where will you go?

Right, where nothing is left and you cannot give anymore of yourself?

Or

Left, where nothing is right and you cannot give the freedom of being yourself?

Stop.

Be Still.

Breathe.

What happens next? What will unfold at this crossroad?

You tell me, I listen.

I am but an echo of your innermost creations.

I cannot escape you and you cannot escape me.

This is our journey, this is your journey and this is my journey.

The whole universe resides within you;
unlimited and endless in its possibilities,
A magic wand to its beholder.

In you lie the tools of the masterpiece, each part steering the course of creation.

The beholder whether aware or not;

is painting the picture in which the canvas gives its identity.

There is no other way I can tell you.

There is no other way I can water the seed.

You are infinite, You are endless, You are unlimited and You are unconditional.

And;
our blessing and curse is that we are connected;
we form a part of a much bigger whole,
this can either elevate us to another level of greatness,
or it can drag us down to levels of unapologetic ignorance.

Know and remember;
the most dangerous matter or energy that keeps holding you back is you.

Know and remember;
Act out your own thoughts and words or you will keep on blaming everything but you in this life.

In order to understand where I'm coming from,
in order to conceive of what I am trying to express,
in order to touch upon how I feel,
you have to take that leap of faith of letting go.

Let go of the construct they have constructed for you.

Lay forth a foundation of your own experience.
Build on it the expressions which you choose to manifest.

Moving like a bicycle; at first you have to peddle ever so much.
Once balanced, you can direct your path with the wand of a thought.

Step by step, learn to come to yourself, arrive at your throne and find your power.

Breathe, linger at the canvas.

You may think, you may say, you may do, you may feel;
but behind all of it is the spirit,
the director of this and that, the driver that decides here or there.
the one deciding if to continue reading or close the book.

Be conscious;

We are dealing with "Godly" matters.

Subtle in the process yet loud in the changes that follow.

Patience is very critical when you begin to come back to yourself.

Yes, it is a beginning;
it is a coming back

and it is all to you.

Now you must begin to observe yourself,
do not be quick to judge yourself,
for long is the journey you are yet to travel.

Do not be quick to praise yourself,
for short is the journey you have travelled.

Lifetimes have you travelled to reach this.

It is not the highest or lowest you have touched upon.
So you need to take baby steps.

Many are invested in you; when you rise to yourself mother
earth rises too;
and when you go below yourself mother earth loses herself too.

Step back and linger, get lost in yourself.

Take a moment and die.

Yes, take this moment and move out of your shelf.

Watch yourself take fear and ride its wings to the beginning of
courage where you shall witness Your true Self.

For a long time you've feared what You are.

Don't get me wrong, there is doubt, but once you've come to the conclusion of all thought,
of all feeling and you have experienced being tired of being tired.
You have for a moment, called forth eternity to dance.

The feeling of being scared often leads ourselves to the vulnerability of external forces created by our own habitual thinking.

Yet remember ;
You are still learning, you are still curious in the steps which you take to know yourself, to know you.

Don't judge yourself for the fall, you've experienced what it means to not be yourself.

Neither should your praise yourself for the rise, you've only touched upon what you truly are.

Day by day we must constantly remind ourselves who we are.

On the "bad" days, we must rise up to our true nature,
on the "good" days, we must ground ourselves to our true being.

For our true nature is being who we are and our true being is naturally who we are.

The world may come with its definitions of who you are, what you are, how you came to be, where you began, when you came to be, and why you are you.

Do not linger and doubt the creation you are,
you may at times look upon other creations and try to compare

Yet;

There is no use trying or seeking to be anything but yourself.

You can only but;
move to being more of you or even less of you yet you cannot not be yourself.

Yet you seem to always put your energy and consciousness on everything but yourself.

Remember this though;

This very self cannot fill cups while itself is empty of the very thing it is trying to pour.

Breathe.

Remind yourself who you are,
Mind yourself to who you are being.

What you have been has created what you are. What you are is creating what you will be.

Breathe.

Remind yourself who you are,
Mind yourself to who you are being.

Courage

Of all things you behold,
Courage must be the one consistent state of being held within.

It takes courage to love;
It takes courage to fear.

It takes courage to be whatever you are being.
The courage to change, and the courage to remain the same are but one expression seeking to experience itself.

This state of being makes one act, and in acting you express, with expression the experience is then manifest.

The world is full of courageous beings,
Whether that courage is being courageously 'stupid' or 'intelligent', ' good' or 'bad',
it is all part of experience expressing itself.

Know this and abide in its wisdom.
For it takes great courage to doubt.

I could keep reminding you of your Sovereignty and you would still doubt.

You keep experiencing your power to create that which manifests, but you still doubt.

All the answers to your questions are but given by the one who asks, yet you still doubt.

For a being to have courage, it has to believe what it knows.

To be alive in what one knows and live it.

For the absence of courage is but the doubt in what one believes to be true.
So much courage you have that you believe another man's journey, yet you doubt the one you are experiencing.

So much courage you have that you live another man's truth, yet you are a spectator to the life unfolding from you.

How else do you expect your experience to unfold?

Slowly my child, slowly.

The Arrival

Remember;
The sun walks side by side with the moon to manifest light in darkness.

All the polarities of this realm are but one journey with many roads.

All your experiences whether 'good' or 'bad' are what we call life in its full manifestation.

And this and that are not different, for they stem from one pole.

This has more this than that
And so
That has more that than this.

Yet remember this and that, is but that and this.

Slowly my child,
Begin to grasp the layout of the game.

The conditions in which you find yourself.

Step back and observe yourself observe.

Stay with the observer.

Now begin to remember;
This is neither that and that is neither this;
Until you begin to cease to observe and start being this and that.

And;
At times, you'll often find yourself at crossroads,
left you look, right you think.
Whatever decision you make will be the effect of whatever causes your will to be.

Look at life like a mirror, observe and reflect what makes you fear the next second.

Sometimes when you are alone, take that slow breath, in and out, as you exhale begin to ponder at the canvas before you, messy and structured, colourful and presence beside you.

You are but a passing wave, you wish, you yearn, you risk, you are the consciousness to whom you have to realize yourself through.

Now;

Stop and linger at your words, for a second watch your thoughts and where they head without your interference.

Do not interfere with the process of life, re-move yourself from the attachment of "being."

Have a taste of "Me," even if it is for a second, a moment you can capture eternally. Watch how you capture it and become chained to its release of freedom in each moment.

That is Me,

Freedom.

The freedom to be.

About The Author

Bonga Makholwa is a self published author who hails from a small town called Matatiele in the Eastern Cape, South Africa.

Born into a loving female dominated family on 11 October 1992, a month and two weeks late, his journey through life begun at his birthplace in Matatiele, life took him to the heart of South Africa (Johannesburg) where he began the process of education.

Coming from the rural areas of the Eastern Cape, going to the tall buildings of Johannesburg, and being in awe of new languages and faces that were new to him, it was an exciting road ahead.

Growing up he has always been the loud mouth, the energy carrier, and the one to bring all together.

This trait was born from the life he found himself in;

From waking up in the great dusty shacks of Jozi and then going to school where that life is a contrast. It taught him humbleness and it the abundance in life at the same time.

After completing the process of education and building of one's character, Bonga had a moment of self-reflection, a moment to rediscover the curiosity of the child which was slowly fading away. It was the first steps of him moving out of his shell.

He wrote his first book 'Thee Truth' which was self published in June 2015.

After that he has been in constant enquiry and application of the truths that came with experience and change.

Offering his thoughts on the journey that lay ahead of the reader, he is publishing his second work My Journey.

www.ingramcontent.com/pod-product-compliance
Lightning Source LLC
LaVergne TN
LVHW041305080426
835510LV00009B/866